Minds Before Market Share

The Art of Public Relations

By

Wayne E. Pollard

authorHOUSE™

1663 Liberty Drive, Suite 200
Bloomington, Indiana 47403
(800) 839-8640
www.AuthorHouse.com

© 2005 Wayne E. Pollard. All Rights Reserved.

No part of this book may be reproduced, stored in a retrieval system, or transmitted by any means without the written permission of the author.

First published by AuthorHouse 09/29/05

ISBN: 1-4208-7821-2 (sc)

Printed in the United States of America
Bloomington, Indiana

This book is printed on acid-free paper.

To my wife,

Ireti,

and my daughters,

Elizabeth and Gabriella

Thus, those skilled in war subdue the enemy's army without battle. They capture his cities without assaulting them and overthrow his state without protracted operations.

Sun Tzu

Table of Contents

Acknowledgments

The following people provided support, ideas, inspiration and encouragement. They deserve special thanks. Ireti Oke-Pollard, Henry and Loretta Pollard, Mark Pollard, Michael Pollard, Henry Vanderlip, Grandmaster Flash, Joe Zucchero, Rich Casey, Bill Casey, Gil Zweig, Kathy Shwiff, Dennis Carmody, Melanie Rigney, Kristin D. Godsey, and Arlene Matthews Uhl.

I am especially grateful to Al Ries, co-author of *The Fall of Advertising and the Rise of PR*. Al encouraged me to write an op-ed piece that was published in *PRWeek*. The feedback I received from that article inspired me to write this book.

Introduction

This is not a "how to" book. You will not learn how to write a press release or how to pitch a story—at least that is not my intention.

Instead, this is a book on what public relations should be if you want to increase sales, more effectively compete in the marketplace, and increase your market share.

Most companies practice public relations (PR) as a post-event activity; they use PR to publicize what has already happened.

- "We won a new client, so let's issue a press release."
- "We are number one in our market, so let's tell everyone about it."

For aggressive firms that are interested in growing, this process is backward. The true value in public relations is in its ability to win minds *before* the sale is made. That's what this book is about: minds before market share. This is the new public relations imperative.

This book is mainly for businesses with direct sales forces. It focuses on PR's strength as being an integral part of a sales attack plan for companies that are aggressively seeking business.

Much emphasis has been placed on PR and ROI (return on investment). Companies traditionally start PR initiatives and sit back and wait for results to come in. They see PR as something that is going to bring them sales by itself. This is incorrect. Public relations can lead to some business; however, it is best used in conjunction with other sales and marketing activities. That is this book's focus.

The best way to win market share is to do it with as little cost (time, money, and personnel) as possible. This is what public relations enables you to do. With public relations, you can win minds first, which then makes it easier to win deals.

Minds Before Market Share: The Art of Public Relations is not a book just for people with the words "public relations" in their job titles; it is for anyone trying to build a brand and create name recognition. It is for anyone who wants to influence the market. It is for anyone who wants to increase market share.

If you are trying to get people to do business with you or to think a certain way about your company or offering, this book is for you. If you are trying to get the media to say positive things about your company, this book is for you. You may be the president of your company, but if you are trying to influence your customers, your prospects, your competitors, or the media, you are a public relations practitioner. This book will provide you with a new understanding of how public relations can help you get sales and increase your market share.

On The Value Of Public Relations

Public relations is the great equalizer. With it, despite your size, you can build your brand and position your company in the minds of your prospects.

Prospects, before your salespeople call on them, will know who you are. They will know your value. Your sales force will win the battle for sales without having to compete. This is the true value of public relations.

Prospects lack time to thoroughly evaluate all options. They rely on companies' positioning and messaging when determining who they should consider doing business with and who they should not.

Thus, through your positioning and messaging, you can get your company included in deals, and your competitors excluded. By getting competitors cut out of deals through your messaging, your prospects defeat your competitors for you.

Credibility is established best through public relations. With it, your salespeople spend less time proving that they are worthy of prospects' business and more time selling. They become more efficient.

With credibility, you can overcome many obstacles, including a lack of funding.

When listing possible vendors, prospects remember those with the most visibility first. Thus, through increased visibility, your salespeople will get into more deals.

Prospects are more comfortable working with companies that are known. They do not want to risk choosing a company with no reputation in the market. They do not want to lose face by choosing an unknown company that fails to deliver.

People are skeptical of advertising; in it, you are saying positive things about yourself. Public relations, however, is getting others to say positive things about you.

If you say it, people question it. If others say it, people believe it. This is the psychology behind public relations.

Through public relations, you can establish your leadership in the market. For most prospects, your position as the leader is the justification they need to do business with you. Few people will question the decision to buy from the leader.

If larger and stronger competitors are successfully implementing public relations campaigns and you follow suit, the market will perceive your firm as larger and stronger than it is in reality. In this way you benefit from the strengths of your competitors.

When you are in dire need of sales and you are faced with funding either public relations or advertising, choose public relations. Cutting public relations to spend on advertising is like a starving woman buying makeup instead of food; she satisfies her vanity but lacks what she needs to survive.

Position your company's leaders as experts in their fields. Many people are swayed by the words of an expert.

Through public relations, you can gain an equal footing with your larger competitors. If you face them in a deal, you will be seen as a worthy competitor despite your size. Competitors of similar size and ability can be made to look less capable and less worthy of winning your prospects' business.

Public relations supplies your sales team with reasons to contact prospects and customers; what good is coverage if people are not told about it?

With credibility and expertise, barriers to sales are removed. "Who are you?" and "why should I work with you?" are questions you no longer hear.

By being positioned as the leader, competing sales teams will have less belief in their ability to win; they will not put forth a great effort to win the deal. Thus, your sales team will face less competition.

In each competitor's customer base, there are those who are more likely to defect than others. Those customers can be influenced to leave your competitor and to do business with you.

Through the media, your competitor's weaknesses can be emphasized while your strengths are promoted. By doing this, you will eat away at a competitor's market share by getting its customers to defect.

Just as you must position your company, you must also position or reposition your competitors. Through your efforts, your competitors lose deals to you even before their salespeople contact prospects. Thus, it is a more effective way of winning deals. This is the acme of public relations skill.

Through the media, the market can be teased; you can build excitement and anticipation of things to come. People will wait on lines to buy from you. They will buy your product before it is available.

Competitors are like thieves trying to steal your market share; they can be warded off with messaging that says you will defend your territory. They will leave you and attack markets that are less protected.

On Public Relations' Primary Purpose

Your objective is to influence people to buy your offerings. This is done by delivering your messaging to those who influence or impact the decision-making process.

Prospects, customers, competitors, and the media must all be influenced. Influence is the primary purpose of public relations.

What is branding but influencing prospects and customers to associate the name of your company or offering with some positive attribute?

Every day, stories are being pitched to the media. They have too little time and too few people on staff to determine, on their own, what should or should not be covered. You must help the media determine what should be covered. This is done by influencing them to tell your story.

Never forget that the media rely on you for news. You provide a service by showing them how your story is newsworthy and how others' stories are not.

Education and communication are not the objective of public relations. Education for what purpose? Communication for what purpose? Education and communication must serve a purpose and that purpose is to influence.

Public relations is part of a combined attack on the market. It prepares the market for your sales attack by winning over as many minds as possible and by warding off your competitors.

Even when your market is not being attacked by a competitor, you still must remind your prospects, customers, and competition of your presence. You must remind them of your leadership position.

Credibility is gained when the media say you are the authority, you are the leader. If you say it, the market will not believe you. If the media say it, the market believes it is the truth.

Education should never be the objective of a public relations campaign. You must do more than provide information. Facts do not move people to action.

Avoid the temptation of trying to change people's minds. Changing minds is a slow and painful process. Influencing people to accept something that does not conflict with an existing belief is far easier.

On Public Relations and Sales

The true power of public relations lies in its ability to help generate sales by influencing buying behavior. Public relations strategy must help companies get new customers or retain their current customers.

Impact on sales is how public relations should ultimately be judged. What difference has the public relations campaign made in the company's ability to generate revenue?

If public relations helps you retain more customers and attack your competitors, it has done its job. If it helps you generate more leads, close more deals, take your competitors' customers, and increase customers' use of your offering, it has done its job.

Too much emphasis is placed on media impressions and not enough is placed on helping generate sales. One million impressions and hundreds of articles mean nothing if sales are unaffected and your company is not positioned properly for success in the market.

A handful of impressions with the right messaging and seen by the right decision makers is more valuable than millions of impressions that do not lead to sales.

Public relations must be viewed as a practice that supports sales. If not, in tough economic times, public relations budgets will continue to get slashed.

If CEOs are not convinced that public relations can help them generate sales, they will cut their public relations budgets.

How will this increase sales? How will this help me keep customers? How will this help me increase my market share? These are the questions that must be answered when evaluating public relations strategy.

Public relations allows you to win sales in the minds of your prospects first. With it, you have already won the battle for customers, even before your salesperson makes the first call.

You must not only win in the minds of your prospects, you must also win the battle in the minds of your competitors. You must instill fear; you must make your competitors believe that you are invincible, that they can not attack your space and win.

By winning the battle in your competitors' minds, they will believe they have lost the deal even before the final decision is made, and they will not work as hard to win the business from you. They lose because of their belief in your superiority.

Public relations helps generate sales by making it easier for your sales team to close deals. When prospects are contacted, they already know who you are and the value you provide. They have already favorably positioned your offering in their minds, making it easier for your sales team to close deals.

The world is filled with too much information. Prospects have less time to devote to thoroughly evaluating options, especially when the issues surrounding the buying decision are complex.

Prospects position you and your competitors, which makes decision making easier. This offering is the fastest, the other is the least expensive, and so on. They rely on the mental shortcuts created by positioning and branding. Help them by positioning your offering for them.

Do not be like those companies that know that they need public relations but say that they must wait until they can afford it at some unknown point in the future. A company that is seeking to gain market share and is challenging a well-funded competitor with a larger sales force can not afford to wait to implement a public relations campaign if it wants to be successful.

No sales campaign should be launched without first preparing the market through public relations. Public relations must be an integral part of any sales campaign. Without it, you are not using all of the sales weapons available to you.

Do not be like those whose public relations departments do not know what their sales departments are doing. The two departments must meet and coordinate their efforts. The messaging promoted by the public relations department and the messaging promoted by the sales department must be the same.

Rarely do public relations professionals meet with the sales team to seek its input. Yet, it is the sales team that has the most contact with the people who we are trying to influence: prospects and customers.

Seek input from the sales team when devising messaging and campaigns. The sales team knows what prospects and customers are saying and thinking. They know why prospects buy. They know the competitions' strengths and weaknesses. They are in the best position to know what messaging will work in the market.

Public relations' job is to play a lead role in determining and promoting your company's positioning and messaging. And public relations must make sure the position and messaging are known and used by sales and marketing. To do this, the head of public relations must sit at the table with the CEO, the head of marketing, and the head of sales.

Why should public relations take the lead in developing the positioning? Public relations' job, more than sales and marketing, is to understand how to influence and persuade the market.

You should seek to affect public opinion toward your company; a good reputation is valuable. However, the focus of public relations must first be to help generate sales.

CEOs should give their views on the state and future of their industries. However, they still must position their companies. Being seen as a thought leader must not help a CEO's ego or the corporation's egos; it must help the company get business.

Seek input from the sales team on the effectiveness of the public relations campaign. They are in the best position to know whether prospects are being influenced.

Do clients know who you are? How are you positioned in their minds? How do they view you and your competitors? Are you viewed as a leader in your market? Your sales team can answer these questions.

In warfare, Psychological Operations (PSYOP) induces or reinforces attitudes and behavior that is favorable to the originator's objectives. In business, public relations is equivalent to PSYOP; it is a form of information warfare.

Public relations is the great equalizer. For the growing company, it is a force multiplier. In the military, a force multiplier is a capability that, when added to and used by a combat force, significantly increases the combat potential of that force and therefore enhances the probability of the mission being successfully accomplished.

Just as PSYOP is a combat force multiplier, public relations is a sales force multiplier.

A sales force multiplier is a capability that, when added to and employed by the sales force, significantly increases the potential of that sales force to get sales and therefore enhances the probability of successfully closing deals.

Public relations prepares the market for your sales troops. As PSYOP does for combat forces, public relations sets the stage for your sales attack and increases the probability of sales success in your market.

In warfare, PSYOP complements the overall conduct of operations. In business, public relations must complement the overall conduct of sales operations. Public relations must contribute to winning the market over to your company.

In warfare, PSYOP enables combat forces to win with a minimum loss of life. In business, public relations must enable sales forces to win market share with minimum loss of dollars and time.

Public relations, when used as a sales force multiplier, is what will enable the smaller company to be victorious when facing a larger competitor with more money, more personnel, and more visibility.

As with PSYOP, public relations can be overt, such as a press tour, or subtle, such as a bylined article. To effectively influence buying behavior, a combination of overt and subtle activities must be used.

As with PSYOP, you must analyze your market's needs, concerns, and desires to determine the best messaging and the best method for delivering your messaging.

PSYOP's objective is to influence behavior so that the enemy gives up or does the conquering force's will without fighting. In using public relations as a sales force multiplier, the objective is to get people to become customers or remain customers without having to fight competitors for the business.

The most effective way to win a war is to do so with as little loss of life as possible. Likewise, the most effective way to win market share is to do so with as little cost as possible: as little time spent, money spent, personnel spent, and effort spent as possible. By winning minds first, public relations enables you to win market share to the point that closing deals is just a formality.

On Strategy and Tactics

To position your firm so that prospects do business with you without considering your competitors is the acme of public relations skill.

Branding is not enough; you must position.

Branding? For what purpose? Branding alone does not lead to sales. Prospects can name many brands, but how many do they buy?

Positioning is more important than branding. A product can be known and still not occupy a space in prospects' minds.

Use a combination of both offensive and defensive public relations. You must acquire new customers while defending your current customer base.

Offensive measures enable you to acquire new customers and attack your competitors; they decrease sales resistance. Defensive measures solidify your position as a provider in the minds of your customers.

Do not attack competitors directly. Instead, let their former customers do the attacking for you in your case studies, press releases, and user groups.

Those skilled in public relations beat their competitors without facing sales resistance. They gain market share without advertising battles and price wars.

When competitors are few and the market is new, position someone in your company as an expert.

When there are many competitors and the market is established, create a new segment and position your company as the leader.

When your competitor has a strong national presence, position your company as the authority in your region.

When competitors are large generalists, position your company as a specialist.

When your public relations team is outnumbered by your competitor's, concentrate your efforts on a segment in which your competitor is vulnerable.

When you have a strong national presence, use your position as a national leader to get regional and local coverage in your markets.

When your competitor is your equal, seek to build better relationships with the media.

If your public relations team is greatly outnumbered, improve team members' efficiency through training.

Build your credibility on a solid foundation. Create a momentum that is difficult for the media to resist.

If your company is unknown, seek local coverage first. Then seek coverage in outlets of increasing size. If your market is geographical, seek local, regional, and then statewide coverage.

If your market is vertical or horizontal, first seek coverage in outlets for that market. Then, seek coverage in the general business press.

Take your competitors' strengths and reposition them. A strong generalist is a weak specialist. Dominance in one vertical market means weakness in another.

Do not validate competitors' messaging by using it in your communications. Reposition competitors based on who their customers really are and the areas in which they truly have expertise and not on what their messaging says.

You can not easily attain leadership in a market that is dominated by several strong and well-positioned competitors. More important than knowing the battles you can win is knowing the battles you cannot win.

A gap exists between your competitor's positioning and reality. Find that gap and exploit it.

The best strategy is to be the first in a new market. The first in a market is automatically positioned as the leader and the leader is assumed to be the best.

Those skilled in public relations find areas in which to be first and do not engage in useless battles with market leaders.

To secure coverage for the market leader is not the acme of public relations skill. To successfully pitch a story that the media must have is not the sign of a public relations expert.

Creating a campaign that is obvious to all is not the acme of skill.

Creating a story where there was none, positioning an unknown company as the leader, creating demand when there was none, obtaining sales without resistance, creating a new market to be first in ... these are the signs of one skilled in public relations.

When creating a new market, quickly establish your position as the first in that market. Otherwise, a competitor with better funding, a larger public relations team, and a position as a leader in an adjacent market could swoop into your new market and, if using great speed, usurp your position as the leader.

Build on your credibility so that it casts a shadow on other areas. People assume that credibility in one area means credibility in adjacent areas.

Companies rarely use enough public relations specialists; they are unaware of the true value that public relations provides. For each market segment, there must be a public relations specialist or team responsible for influencing that market.

Having an insufficient public relations force is like fighting a war without enough troops. You must supply ample manpower to the effort.

Have enough public relations specialists to take advantage of the opportunities in your markets. Have enough to support your company's sales efforts.

Align your efforts with your company's objectives. Too often, public relations says one thing, sales another, and marketing another.

On Messaging

Public relations tools do not fail; it is the messaging that fails to influence the market.

Messaging must be geared to either help acquire customers or keep customers. This is done through positioning and branding.

All of your communications must support your positioning. No communication should be in vain.

Messaging must do more than just provide facts. People will not read or hear your information and make rational decisions in favor of your offering. Decisions are made based on emotions and then, later, rationalized with facts.

In warfare, PSYOP is used to give the enemy false impressions, such as the existence of many troops in an area where there are none. Likewise, in public relations, use your messaging to lead your competitors to believe that you are stronger than you are.

It is much easier to position yourself as a leader in a market that you have created than to attempt to position yourself as a leader in an existing market.

Position yourself as an authority. People have a strong tendency to obey authority.

On Media Relations

Do not manipulate or abuse the media. The coverage you gain today is not worth the friends you will lose tomorrow.

Studying is the key to securing coverage. Study the content. Study the audience and its needs. Study what your competitors have said and done. Study how the piece you will pitch has been covered in the past two years. Only after much studying will you be able to pitch with above-average success.

Like a Major League pitcher, you must know to whom you are pitching. What pitches are preferred? What is needed? What is desired? Information is easily accessible. Do not insult a member of the media by pitching an inappropriate story.

Your objective is to help the media do their jobs. Do not be like the selfish friend who only thinks of his needs. Instead, think first about how you can help the media meet their needs. This is the key to successful media relations.

The media are not your enemies. The media are not your friends. They are a neutral state whose interest is in the story. The media treat you like an enemy or a friend, contingent upon how it helps the story.

With the media, until you are a trusted source, the story has precedence over the relationship. Once you have proven your value, the relationship has precedence over the story—for a time.

See the media as having a scale, constantly weighing the relationship with you versus the story. In the less desirable case, your objective is to make sure that the two are balanced; you will get fair coverage.

When the relationship is more valuable than the story, the story will still be covered; however, you will have a sympathetic ear. You will have ample opportunity to present your side of the story. This is the ideal relationship.

Do not send press releases that are not newsworthy. This information is useless and is thrown out. Sending useless information under the pretext of keeping your company's name in the minds of the media is a waste of the media's time.

Put yourself in a box. The media seeks to categorize your company and your offering. Clearly define both so that they can either be put into an existing category or put into categories that you have created. If you do not put yourself in a box, you will have great difficulty getting out of the one that the media put you in.

The media's job is to get the story. Your job is to get your message out. Have a message and get it out at every opportunity.

Preparation is the key to a successful interview. Know the interviewer's intentions. Anticipate questions and have answers prepared. Expect the unexpected and prepare for that as well. Prepare to the point that nothing can surprise you.

Do not attempt to deceive the media. It is better to say "I don't know" than to say "I know" and be proven wrong. Your lack of knowledge will soon be forgotten, but your deception will always be remembered.

When speaking of the competition, be subtle in your communication. Competition must be positioned or repositioned, but not overtly attacked.

Never bash the competition. This reveals your fear of your competition and makes the media inquisitive; they will want to know if your fear is justified. This fear will then be conveyed to the market.

Never boast. Promote your message and position your company, but be humble in your accomplishments. Being boastful and arrogant only invites the media to find your faults.

On Using Public Relations

Do not be like those who sit back and wait for the dividends of their public relations campaigns to come in. Public relations is not a passive investment; you must work hard to get a return.

As with farming, you plant your positioning in the minds of the market and you watch it grow. Then, your sales team must go and reap the rewards of your effort.

Waiting for sales to come in after your campaign is like waiting for apples to fall off a tree; some apples will fall, but the majority must be picked.

Before your sales team presents your offering, the salespeople must first establish your credibility in the market. This is done by showing prospects the results of your public relations campaign. In this way, sales resistance will be decreased.

Teach your sales team how to use public relations tools. Case studies create social pressure. Interviews in leading media outlets build credibility. Bylined articles establish authority. A tool is useless if you do not know how to use it.

On the Problem with Public Relations

The original intent of public relations in business was to influence buying behavior. Yet today, definitions of "public relations" omit this and focus instead on building relationships. What good are relationships if they do not effect sales?

Relationship building should not be the objective of public relations campaigns. How will these relationships directly help generate revenue? This must be asked. Building relationships must be done with the objective of generating revenue in mind.

Too much emphasis is placed on media impressions and not enough is placed on sales. One million impressions and hundreds of articles mean nothing if sales are unaffected and the company is not positioned properly.

Public relations specialists are too content with campaigns that only boost egos. You can either boost your ego or boost your sales.

Position or be positioned is the law of the public relations jungle. Yet too many public relations specialists violate this law. They become victims of the positioning imposed on them by their competitors and the media.

Too much emphasis is placed on reputation management. For the growing company with limited resources, generating sales and positioning are more important. Many companies with good reputations have failed from lack of sales.

Establishing a good reputation must not be the primary goal. Public relations must do more than just build a good reputation; it must influence buying behavior.

Public relations specialists complain of not being invited to the C-level meetings. They must spend less time focusing on their inability to meet with C-level executives and more time establishing their ability to support the company's objectives. Public relations must position itself as a practice that adds significant value to the company.

What is valued most by clients is media relations. Yet too often this most important task is given to the least experienced people while those with the most experience focus on strategic planning. Strategic planning is useless without having experienced people who can effectively execute the plan.

Every day, editors receive press releases that have no news value. Issuing press releases that are not newsworthy for the sake of keeping your company's name before the media is a waste of your time and, more importantly, the media's.

No coverage is better than useless coverage; you get the same results without wasting money.

How will this interview impact sales? How will speaking at this event help gain or retain customers? How will writing this article help position the company? These are questions that must be answered.

Conclusion

Throughout military history, superior strategy has enabled many smaller forces to defeat larger ones. Likewise, in the battle for market share, smaller companies can defeat larger, better-funded competitors if they have a superior public relations strategy.

Before you begin your public relations campaign you must ask yourself one important question: what is my objective?

Do you want to increase your market share? Do you want to decrease sales resistance? If you truly do, then with every tactic and every piece of communication ask yourself: how does this help our positioning? How does this help decrease sales resistance? How does this help us win minds?

Your answers should be clear and scientific. Although public relations is an art, it is an art that is based on a science: psychology.

With a limited budget, you can grow if you are willing to make sacrifices. You must be willing to sacrifice short-term strokes of the ego for long-term market share gains. You must be willing to replace useless activity with real productivity.

You must be willing to put aside your previous beliefs about what public relations is and focus on what it can be. And you must be willing to give up keeping up with the corporate Joneses by indiscriminately trying to get your name in any and every media outlet, and only pursue coverage that helps you with your overall objective, which is to increase market share.

You can either boost your ego or boost your market share. The choice is yours.

Bibliography

Bernays, Edward. *Propaganda*. With an introduction by Mark Crispin Miller. Brooklyn, NY: Ig Publishing, 2005.

Cialdini, Robert B. *Influence: Science and Practice,* 4th ed. Boston: Allyn and Bacon, 2001.

Lawrence, T. E. *Seven Pillars of Wisdom: A Triumph*. New York: Anchor Books, 1991. First printed by M. Pike, 1926.

Liddell Hart, B. H. *Strategy,* 2nd revised ed. New York: Meridian, 1967.

Pratkanis, Anthony and Elliot Aronson. *Age of Propaganda: The Everyday Use and Abuse of Persuasion,* revised ed. New York: W.H. Freeman, 2001.

Ries, Al and Laura Ries. *22 Immutable Laws of Branding: How to Build a Product or Service into a World-Class Brand*. New York: HarperBusiness, 1998.

Ries, Al and Laura Ries. *The Fall of Advertising and the Rise of PR*. New York: HarperBusiness, 2002.

Senger, Harro von. *The Book of Stratagems: Tactics for Triumph and Survival*. Ed. and trans. by Myron B. Gubitz. New York: Viking, 1991.

Trout, Jack and Steve Rivkin. *The New Positioning: The Latest on the World's #1 Business Strategy*. New York: McGraw-Hill, 1996.

Tzu, Sun. *The Art of War*. Trans. by Samuel B. Griffith. Oxford: Oxford University Press, 1963

Yano, Shin'ichi. *New Lanchester Strategy*. Sunnyvale, Calif.: Lanchester Press, 1995-1996.

About the Author

Wayne E. Pollard is president of Hunter-Pollard, a management consulting firm that uses its proprietary process, Engineering Demand™, to position clients and build their brands. Pollard has over fifteen years of public relations, sales, and marketing experience. As a consultant to public relations and advertising firms, he has worked on the campaigns of industry leading companies, helping clients get exposure in media outlets including *Computerworld, Wall Street & Technology,* and MTV.

Pollard was the president and cofounder of the first online career site for experienced diversity job seekers. Pollard generated coverage for the site in publications such as *The Boston Globe, Fortune Small Business, Entrepreneur, CBSMarketWatch,* and *Human Resource Executive,* successfully positioning the company as one of the top three diversity career sites.

Pollard's articles, under his own byline and as a ghostwriter, have appeared in publications including *The New York Times, The Village Voice, PR Week, Writer's Digest, Chief Information Officer, Computerworld Australia, Darwin, Inside Direct Mail, The Deal, Wall Street & Technology, Financial Executive, American Banker, FedTech, Wireless Week, Wireless Business & Technology, NJBIZ,* the *Asbury Park Press,* the *Daily Record,* and others. He has been interviewed by such media outlets as *The San Jose Mercury News,* USAToday.com, CBSMarketWatch, "The Dolans," and CNBC TV's "Power Lunch."

You may reach Pollard at wepollard@hunterpollard.com.

www.ingramcontent.com/pod-product-compliance
Lightning Source LLC
Chambersburg PA
CBHW021901170526
45157CB00005B/1922

* 9 7 8 1 4 2 0 8 7 8 2 1 9 *